CHOOSING A SMALL MAMMAL

INTRODUCTION

If you care to browse any pet books in a store you will find there are general reference works on dogs, cats, birds, fish, reptiles, amphibians—even spiders. What you will rarely see is a reference book devoted to small mammalian pets. There is an assumption that where these critters are concerned a potential pet owner knows exactly what sort of companion they want.

While this may be true for many potential owners, this still leaves a lot of people who are not sure which small mammal would be the best to keep indoors as a house pet. This book was written specifically for this group of people. But its value is not restricted to this group. Today, more than ever before, many households are multi-pet owners.

Rather than consult numerous books on each of the small mammals they own, they may appreciate a work that gives all the important information in one concise volume. In the following chapters every one of the highly popular small mammalian pets are discussed—from a suitability standpoint, and in relation to their welfare needs.

Additionally, a few of the less common pets are included. One or more of these may, in the next few years, emerge from being 'exotic', and somewhat rare to become highly popular. They may follow in the wake of the hedgehog and sugar glider. Both of these, especially the hedgehog, emerged from total obscurity to become, in just a few years, much loved and highly popular pets.

The initial chapters are devoted to a general discussion of important subjects—choosing, housing, and feeding. These are followed by chapters on each of the major small pets. Finally, a general chapter on health care approximate for all small pets is included.

The more important information on the many species discussed is summarized at the end of the book to provide a quick reference source. To overcome the need for lengthy descriptions of the species, all of the popular ones are lavishly illustrated in full color to create not only comprehensive information, but also a pictorial feast.

Once you have decided on the pet best suited for your home, you are strongly advised to purchase a book devoted to the care of that pet. This is especially important where the newer popular pets are concerned, such as the hedgehog and sugar glider.

Distributed in the UNITED STATES to the Pet Trade by T.F.H. Publications, Inc., One T.F.H. Plaza, Neptune City, NJ 07753; on the Internet at www.tfh.com; in CANADA Rolf C. Hagen Inc., 3225 Sartelon St. Laurent-Montreal Quebec H4R 1E8; Pet Trade by H & L Pet Supplies Inc., 27 Kingston Crescent, Kitchener, Ontario N2B 2T6; in ENGLAND by T.F.H. Publications, PO Box 15, Waterlooville PO7 6BQ; in AUSTRALIA AND THE SOUTH PACIFIC by T.F.H. (Australia), Pty. Ltd., Box 149, Brookvale 2100 N.S.W., Australia; in NEW ZEALAND by Brooklands Aquarium Ltd. 5 McGiven Drive, New Plymouth, RD1 New Zealand; in SOUTH AFRICA, Rolf C. Hagen S.A. (PTY.) LTD. P.O. Box 201199, Durban North 4016, South Africa; in Japan by T.F.H. Publications, Japan—Jiro Tsuda, 10-12-3 Ohjidai, Sakura, Chiba 285, Japan. Published by T.F.H. Publications, Inc.

MANUFACTURED IN THE
UNITED STATES OF AMERICA
BY T.F.H. PUBLICATIONS, INC.

Ferrets are playful and inquisitive creatures. When choosing a ferret as a pet be prepared for plenty of mischief!

CONTENTS

Hamsters

Hedgehogs

Chinchillas

Sugar Gliders

Guinea Pigs

Rabbits

PHOTOGRAPHS BY
Joan Balzarini, M. Gilroy, Isabelle Francais, Ralph Lehrmayer, Robert Percy, Vincent Serbin, Louise van der Meid.

The rabbit is the most popular small sized pet in the world. A whole new hobby is developing around the diminutive forms such as this Netherland Dwarf.

CHOOSING THE RIGHT PET

Selection of the right pet for your home requires answers to the following three major questions.

• What is the legal status of the pets that may be on your initial selection list? Which ones can legally be kept in your residential district?

• Which will be most suited to your particular needs and situation?

• Which factors are the most important when actually purchasing a pet?

A PET'S LEGAL STATUS

Years ago, most small mammals you might have wanted to keep as pets were not subject to many regulations. The situation has changed dramatically. In recent years interest in exotic or pocket pets has expanded rapidly.

The laws today are so complex that categoric statements about the legality of keeping any of the small mammals would be impossible when applied internationally, or even regionally within countries. Therefore, it becomes impossible to give specific guidelines on legislation.

The following guidelines are general, which is not to say they necessarily apply to where you live. Each pet owner is responsible for establishing the legality of owing any of the pets in this book.

Rabbits, guinea pigs (cavies), hamsters, gerbils, mice, rats and ferrets are regarded by most nations as traditional, long established, domestic pets. As such, they are usually free of the controlling regulations that some other potential pets are subject to (gerbils and ferrets being the more dubious in status in some countries).

Other pets may be legal within a country, but they may not be at a regional level (e.g., state, territory). Even if legal within a state, they may be illegal at county or town

When choosing a pet it is important to consider whether or not the pet's needs will be compatible with yours. Hamsters are notoriously easy to care for and undemanding.

Guinea pigs are one of the larger small pets. As such, they will need to spend ample time outside their living quarters.

level. All pets are of course subject to regulations regarding their general welfare, and most are also subject to special regulations that control breeding.

This means that while you may keep one or two rabbits in a home as pets, the number may be subject to an upper limit beyond which you cannot exceed or which will require a special permit.

Where non-traditional pets are concerned, do not rely on what a breeder, pet store, or vet tells you in respect to the legality of a given species. They may not be up to date on the current position. At times, the situation is so confusing that even those who implement the laws—

governmental departments— are not always sure, species to species, what the legislation is. The advice must therefore be that you check with your local Department of Wildlife, Department of Agriculture, Department of Natural Resources, or whichever other governmental body is responsible for implementing the laws related to species which may be kept as pets in your area. It is also advised that you check with your local town hall.

You are advised to not keep any species that is illegal in your country, or residential area. The fines may be severe, and your pets may be confiscated. Furthermore, by so doing you merely provide

more ammunition to those pressure groups that wish to see all pet keeping banned or more strictly regulated.

WHICH PET IS PERFECT FOR YOU

Selecting the best pet for a given circumstance embraces many aspects that differ from one home to another. Some pets will be living with a single owner, others within a family comprising of adults and children of various ages. In the single owner situation, no consideration of other people is a factor. But in a family situation it can be very important.

A distinction should be made between the larger small pets, such as rabbits,

Arguably the hardiest of all small pets, gerbils gained popularity in the early 1950s. Exceptionally clean, and one of the most gentle rodents, they make excellent pets.

guinea pigs, hedgehogs, and sugar gliders, and those which are basically cage pets—mice, hamsters and the like. The larger pet should be given ample free-roaming time in the home, whether this be restricted to certain rooms or not. This will involve some fecal matter being deposited

obtained for children unless a parent, or other mature family member, is prepared to accept total responsibility for his welfare.

Children can be very neglectful of a pet once its initial novelty has worn thin. They must be educated in handling and caring for the

good choice. You should obtain a companion for him. Most small caged pets are equally subject to loneliness, the popular hamster being an unusual exception.

The best general advice you can take with regards to the choice of a small pet is this: Read each of the chapters on

Most pets are social animals, like these mice, who need the companionship of their owners to live full lives.

on floors, and may involve some nibbling of carpets or furniture.

If this would upset you to the point that it resulted in the pet being relegated to a life in his small housing (any housing will be small to these larger pets), then such pets would not be an ideal choice. Nor should any pet be

pet, and any abuse should be disciplined. If a responsible person cannot do this, then no pets should be kept.

Most pets are social animals, so consideration to how much time is available to be spent with them is important. A single rabbit or guinea pig that will be left alone for long periods is not a

the various pets, and think of all the problems that might occur. If these do not present any problems to you, then the pet should be suited to your needs.

If you are prepared to accept any likely problems, you can assume you will be happy with your choice. Too many people focus only on the

It is important to check all state and local laws before purchasing any pet. Although certain pets may gain popularity, sometimes they cannot be kept legally in all states.

The health of an animal is a very important consideration when it comes time to make your purchase. This rat's coat is shiny, and he is alert and active—all signs of a healthy pet.

cute or nice aspects of a pet, only to be disappointed when they find the pet has potential drawbacks—every pet has these. Essentially, the smaller the pet, the less likely it is to present problems.

No animal is a perfect pet, because no animal was meant to live with humans. Pet ownership must be a two way street. Like it or not, the pet has to accept your shortcomings; in turn you must accept any that might come with a given species.

FACTORS TO CONSIDER WHEN SELECTING A PET

The most important factors in purchasing any pet are those concerning health, temperament, and age. Its color, though this may be important to you, should never override the other three factors. The source of the pet is important as it may have a bearing on both the health and quality of the pet. Cost will normally only be a factor in the more exotic species.

Health

There is little point in having the most beautiful of pets if he is not healthy. Very small mammals are not easy to treat for major problems, so you must have a fit individual. The health of an animal is often apparent at the time of purchase. However there may be a problem in its early stages that has not yet manifested itself.

Assessment of what cannot be seen must be made by the seller's reputation, and the way the pets are being kept. If conditions are cramped, overcrowded, and dirty, with no evidence of regular cleaning and feeding (dirty water containers, no dry food to be seen in the housing) you should assume there is a strong possibility the pet may have a developing problem.

Visual evidence of a pet's health is obvious. He should be lively, with clear eyes, no discharge of mucous from eyes or nose, no signs of hair loss, swellings or abrasions, nor any problems related to mobility. Carefully read the health chapter before purchasing any pet.

Temperament

Regardless of age, any pet should have a docile nature. If the seller cannot easily handle the animal, you are better off looking elsewhere. Even a small mammal, such as a hamster or mouse, can inflict a painful bite. The onus for hand-taming a pet should be with the seller, not the pet owner.

Age

Most small pets are not especially long lived. To obtain maximum pleasure from your ownership of them, it is desirable to acquire them when they are young. This gives you the added advantage that youngsters are more readily tamed. The more mature individual may not achieve the same level of training if he was not handled from an early age.

The Source

All of the pets in this book can be obtained from pet shops. As long as the store maintains high standards of cleanliness and meets other needs they should be an ideal place to purchase your pet. The pets should be housed by sex, never mixed with other species or housed in a location that would be stressful to them.

For example, nocturnal species should not be housed where there is intense lighting. The seller should be able to tell you all about the species. The pet shop, unlike other sources, will be able to supply all of your present and future needs, and so has a vested interest in your being satisfied from the outset.

Never purchase a pet from open markets or similar locations. This displays total disregard for a pet's health. In

The temperament of a pet is very important. If handled correctly, and from an early age, hedgehogs will be sociable creatures who enjoy human contact.

Charming, playful, and entertaining, the chinchilla is actually an endangered species in the wild. First bred for their valuable pelts, chinchillas have become sought-after pets.

some species, the more exotic pet may not be available locally. In this instance, travel to the nearest place that has a good pet shop, or specialist breeder.

Purchasing pets via mail-order can be risky business because you are buying sight unseen. There are a lot of honest breeders and dealers—but there are also unscrupulous individuals. Unless you are very sure of the seller's reputation, caution is strongly advised.

Purchasing unusual species from exotic animal auctions is not recommended to potential pet owners. The key factors in buying a pet is that you can see him, handle him, and see the conditions he is living under before you

part with your money. When you cannot, you greatly increase the risk of dissatisfaction.

Cost

Most of the pets in this book are relatively low cost. However, in the more unusual pets, (the hedgehog, sugar glider, and even dwarf hamsters) beware of claims related to size or color for which a high price is being asked. Many of the claims are unfounded and merely represent a natural variation in the color or the size of the species. Or they may represent aberrant forms resulting from a physiological problem. In such instances they will not breed to their type, they are one-offs.

If the claim is dwarfism, the individual may suffer from problems as it matures. Leave the higher priced unusual forms to the breeders who should be aware of the gable they take when purchasing such individuals. Colors, such as albino, white or black, may well be genuine mutations. When they first appear in a species they command high prices. However, those prices usually start to fall dramatically within a relatively short period of time (1-2 years). Be aware of this if you are thinking of investing in an unusual pet of a new color. The pet owner is best advised to select from the popular forms, which will be the most competitively priced.

Your Pet's Home

You should obtain your pet's housing before your bring your pet home. If your rush the process by buying the house and the pet on the same day, you may regret it.

Many small pets have similar housing needs, and all pets require certain common features within their accommodations. Today, there is a wide range of commercial housing for pets both in styles and costs. Generally, you will get what you pay for, so the first advice is to obtain the best you can afford. Indeed, it is better to save for a preferred house-type than to purchase a lower cost model that will not give either the same pet comfort levels, or last as long.

You should, in most instances, obtain the housing before the pet is purchased. This allows you time to locate just the right model, and have it all fitted out in readiness for the pet. If you rush the process, buying the house and the pet on the same day, you may regret

it later. Much will depend on your budget, and what range of housing and pets your local store has.

BASIC HOUSING CONSIDERATIONS

A pet's home must consist of a number of features. It can

never be too large, but it can certainly be too small. If a pet will be given a lot of free roaming exercise in your home then his housing will only be his sleeping area. It must be larger if the pet will spend many hours each day in its cage. A home should be secure, easy to clean, and offer easy access for you to lift the pet out of his cage.

Security

A cage for a hamster, rat, chinchilla, degu, or similar rodent with powerful incisor teeth needs to be able to withstand its potentially destructive capability. This means that wood or thin plastics are inappropriate materials for these species.

Consideration of the pet's size is also a factor where small species are concerned. For example, bars of commercial cages must be close enough together to

All pets require certain common features in their accommodations. Easy access to food and water are among the most important.

Aquarium style homes provide the advantages of easy viewing and cleaning, security, and are available in an extensive range of sizes.

prevent pets from squeezing through them and escaping. Likewise, in the aquarium style home, a hood (canopy), or a very small hole size mesh, should be fitted to ensure the pet cannot jump out. Solid hoods must feature a number of small ventilation holes.

Housing Materials

All housing should be easy to clean. In this case, wood is not a wise choice. The options are plastic, thermoplastic, sheet metal, weld wire, or a combination of these. Bear in mind that low grade plastics have a short life. Their surfaces soon lose easy-clean capability. They become scratched, and urine can degrade the surface, both staining it, and removing its original smooth coating. Thinly painted sheet metal surfaces may become rusty, while unpolished weld wire is more difficult to keep clean.

Accessibility

The easier it is for you to place your hand in the housing the easier it will be to keep it clean, as well as lift your pet out. Doors should be as large as possible. The door may be top or side opening. In more costly units, an entire panel can be opened, providing much better access. In some units the entire top can be removed from the base to make cleaning easier, and some cages are even fitted with sliding floor traps.

Risk of Injury

Always check that any housing is free of sharp projections that could injure your pet. Cages made from weld wire have become very fashionable. They are low cost and offer a vast range of styles and sizes. Some commercial cages are fitted with false weld wire floors, so the pet is not walking on detritus and fecal matter.

Weld wire walls can be dangerous to small pets, especially those that can climb. The rat and the hedgehog are especially vulnerable to injury in such cages. In either case, the nails, or the entire foot—even the leg—can get trapped in

the wire as the pet attempts to descend. At the least the pet may sprain its foot; at the worst the limb could be broken.

Wire weld floors are not suitable for any pet. They can create sores, are uncomfortable surfaces, and legs can get caught in them resulting in injury. If an otherwise suitable commercial cage features a wire weld floor, you can obtain plastic pet rugs to cover it. But they are not very effective with pets such as rats and hedgehogs, as they can easily tear them and pull them out of place. A fitted solid plastic cover would take care of the problem better.

Slats, made from plastic, are an excellent alternative to mesh floors for rabbits, guinea pigs, and similar sized species. They offer the advantages of mesh floors, but are much more comfortable, and are now featured in a number of commercial hutches and cages.

HOUSING STYLES

There are many styles of pet homes, some better than others. Small rodents, such as mice, hamsters, gerbils, and others of similar size, can be kept in commercial small mammal cages or in aquariums.

The aquarium style home is in many ways still the superior housing for small mammals. It provides the advantages of easy viewing and cleaning, security without risk of injury, and an extensive range of sizes. The tube and tub style homes designed originally for hamsters can be used for

ther burrowing species, but
care must be taken that the
tubes are suitably sized,
neither being too small nor
too large for the pet to move
from one location of the set-
up to another.

Where arboreal species
re concerned, such as the
sugar glider, chinchilla,
possum, and ferret, the
housing should be tall
enough so exercise branches
or resting areas can be
provided. The larger finch
bird cages may be very
suitable for such pets, but
be sure the distance between
the bars is narrow enough to
prevent escape. Hedgehogs
should be kept in a large
aquarium style home. Some
commercial units are now

produced for hedgehogs, but
avoid those with all wire
floors and walls.

FLOOR COVERING

All housing for pets will
require a floor covering to
soak up urine, and provide a
suitable substrate for the pet
to walk on. Although the
options are many, a number
of them have definite
drawbacks. The following
offers a brief summary of the
options.

Wood shavings are
probably the most commonly
used material; those which
contain phenols (found in
pine trees) can have an
adverse effect on the
respiratory and other
systems. In particular,

shavings from cedar trees
should be avoided.

Sawdust can irritate the
respiratory tract, and clings to
the anal region, as well as to
moist foods. Straw has little
absorbency, and its sharp
ends can be dangerous to the
eyes of mammals. Hay is
better, but must be very clean
and fresh. If not, there is an
increased risk it will contain
fungal and other spores which
will mature if dampened.
Garden soil may contain
legions of dangerous
pathogens (disease causing
organisms), while sand is too
abrasive. Clay cat litters can
cause respiratory infections.

Plain white or colored paper
is much safer, and relatively
low cost, but soon looks

Many types of housing and bedding are available for small mammals. Be sure to choose an appropriately-sized cage for your pet and use bedding that is easy to clean.

Housing for your pets will require some sort of floor covering to soak up urine as well as to provide a comfortable surface for walking.

contain dangerous wire and pins within them. If exposed serious injuries could follow. Carefully study the construction of any accessory placed into your pet's home. If in doubt the accessory should not be used.

Safe accessories include twigs and small branches from fruit or other non-poisonous trees. These are good for the pet's teeth, and provide enjoyment. Wooden thread bobbins, and the cardboard from kitchen or toilet rolls, also make wonderful toys and will cost you nothing. Small rocks and logs (washed and rinsed first) look natural and are safe. There are also a variety of commercial accessories that you can add to your pet's home.

Exercise wheels are often appreciated by smaller mammals, but do be sure the size is suited to your species. If the pet has a long tail, check that when the wheel rotates it will not trap the pet's tail.

WHERE TO PLACE YOUR PET'S HOME

The location of a pet's housing in your home is of great importance. Avoid any location that is exposed to long hours of direct sunlight. This will create high temperatures that may go well beyond the comfort level, risking heat stress or exhaustion. Also, housing shouldn't be subject to cold drafts. Nor should accommodations be located on, or in front, of heaters or air conditioning units. Any of these locations may result in rapid temperature changes

A highly-absorbent bedding material will make cleanup easier and reduce odor.

unsightly so must be changed daily. By far the best floor materials are the commercially prepared natural fibers and recycled paper chips and granules. These are non-toxic, rarely dangerous if swallowed, dust free, have high absorbency, and are readily biodegradable.

However, they are rather more expensive than the other alternatives. The advantages greatly outweigh the disadvantages of the other choices, which are best used only in emergencies.

INTERIOR DECORATION OF YOUR PET'S HOME

The range of accessories and toys produced these days for pets is enormous. However, be careful what you choose, as some can be dangerous to your pet. Thin plastic or rubber accessories may be swallowed and could create a serious or fatal digestive system blockage. Cuddly fabric toys may

It is very important that you provide a habitat well suited to your pet's needs. This sugar glider cage is tall and well stocked with foliage to allow for the expression of the animal's natural behavior.

that will cause health problems for your pet.

Do not place housing too close to the floor, especially if larger animals reside in the home. Large animals peering into the cage will cause undue stress to the poor little creature. Air is also colder at ground level, subjecting the pet to uncomfortable temperatures.

In summary, obtain the best home you can for your pet. All pets are very active creatures. They no more enjoy being confined in small cramped conditions than you would. Look for a large, comfortable, and affordable home for your pet. And always think about his health and happiness before you purchase his house.

Be sure to put your pet's housing in a place where the temperature will not fluctuate too greatly. He will not be intimidated by larger pets, but will be easily included in family activities.

Outdoor habitats are only appropriate for some small mammals. Make sure you understand all the requirements of this lifestyle before committing a pet to life outdoors.

FEEDING YOUR PET

Feed your pet a variety of fresh foods to find out what it prefers. Check with your veterinarian to be sure your pet is getting proper nutrition.

All animals fall into broad categories concerning nutritional needs. Herbivores are plant eaters, carnivores are flesh-eaters, omnivores eat both vegetation and meat, and insectivores are invertebrate eaters. This does not mean a species cannot belong to more than one category. You should reflect this knowledge in his diet. An animal may require certain nutrients from foods that are not contained in their primary group, making a balanced diet very important.

MENU CHOICES

Nourishment can take many forms. The moisture content of a food may range from low to high. The constituent value may be biased towards proteins, fats, carbohydrates or vitamins. It may be a commercial food formulated to meet the known nutritional requirements of a particular animal group or specific species.

You are recommended to feed your pet a mixture of each of these. By doing so you minimize the risk that anything will be missing from your pet's diet. Let us consider the reasons for adopting such a philosophy.

First, all natural foods, such as plants, vegetables and fruits, contain different constituents in different quantities. The more limited the range supplied, the greater the possibility one or more ingredients may be missing, or not being supplied in the correct amount.

Secondly, while commercially formulated diets may contain all known needed nutrients, the fact is no one knows what the exact requirements are for any species. Further, some formulations are better than others. The term "complete diet" is only as good as the research and preparation standards that go into its production. This varies from one manufacturer to another.

Finally, while a diet may meet an animal's metabolic needs it may not do so from a psychological standpoint. Animals have a need to be selective in what foods they eat. The selection and eating process maintains the pet's interest in food, thus

You should offer your pet a nutritionally balanced diet, formulated to meet his individual needs. Be sure you allow your pet some variation from time to time to keep things interesting.

providing mental stimulation. When this mental (psychological) aspect is denied the pet, it may result in nutritional stress. Its evolved feeding needs are no longer natural, and this may effect its temperament, as well as its health.

SUDDEN DIET CHANGES

Sudden changes in diet will invariably result in problems.

This is because the bacteria that break down the various food items are specialized in coping with certain constituents. When the form of the food suddenly changes, or is increased, there may be insufficient bacteria present in the system to allow digestion to take place at its normal rate—it may be slowed down, or increased. This is when problems are encountered.

For these reasons a diet should be both varied in its content, yet reasonably stable in the ratio of foods. If changes are deemed necessary these should be made gradually, meaning 7-14 days with the very small pets, and about twice this time for those as large as a rabbit. This gives the digestive system ample time to adjust.

Always establish a pet's diet at the time of purchase, and maintain this during the initial settling-in time. Changing homes is always a traumatic experience for a pet. The more stable you can keep things at this time, the less likely he will suffer from stress.

WATER

Fresh water should be available to your pets on a free choice basis at all times. The amount it will normally drink will be influenced by the amount of moisture in its food contains. If this is high, as in fruits and vegetables, it will drink less than if the diet is mainly in a dry form, such as seeds, grain, pellets or similar foods.

If gravity-fed bottles are the source of the water supply be sure the pet is already familiar with this type of

Do not change your pet's diet too suddenly; it may result in digestive problems.

source. If not, provide an open dish as well. Purchase water bottles fitted with a non-drip spout. Those with graduated measurements are also useful because you can establish how long it takes for the pet to drink a given quantity. Changes in the consumption rate may suggest either the ball bearing in the spout is jammed, or that the pet is not well.

The amount of food a pet consumes should reflect the nutritional content of the food. Dry foods are very concentrated, so a smaller amount of these foods will be necessary than would be the case with moist foods. Also, foods with a high fat or protein content will satiate a

Fresh water should be available to your pets on a free-choice basis at all times.

Foods should be supplied in two dishes: one for dry foods, the other for fresh foods. Fresh foods perish after a time and should be removed.

Always provide fresh water for your pet. Some owners prefer to use a gravity-fed water bottle instead of a water bowl.

pet quicker than those which are mainly composed of carbohydrates. If the diet is too rich in fats the pet will tend to eat these first, because fats provide flavor. Having satiated itself on these, it may then ignore other foods, and the valuable nutrients they contain. This habit could cause problems such as obesity. A balanced diet is a crucial aspect of planned feeding regimens.

Foods should be supplied in two dishes. One for dry foods, the other for fresh foods. Choose heavy pots, or metal ones that are clipped to the side of the housing. These will not be thrown about the cage, or bitten, as will those made of plastic.

FOOD QUANTITY

It can be very difficult to decide how much a pet should eat. Many factors including level of activity, age, breeding state (as in a pregnant or nursing female), current health, temperature of environment, nutritional value of the food items, as well as a pet's individual metabolism influence this.

Taking all factors into account, a healthy pet will normally eat only what it needs to meet its metabolic requirements. Based on this, the following is a good means of establishing how much food is required.

The diet should be divided between dry foods and fresh or soft foods (those with high moisture content). Give a quantity of food to the pet, preferably on the generous side. After about one hour inspect the food dishes.

If a lot of fresh food remains, the amount of these can be reduced at the next meal. Whatever isn't eaten should be disposed of; fresh foods sour quickly. However, if there is food left, the amount should be slightly increased at the next meal. There should always be some dry food left. If not, increase the quantity at the next meal. If there is a lot leftover this should remain in its container, accessible to the animal for up to 24 hours.

This trial and error method should help you establish the quantity of food your pet will consume within a day or two. The general health and

Many factors should be considered when deciding the quantity to feed your pet. Age, activity level, reproductive state, health, environment, and metabolism all play a role.

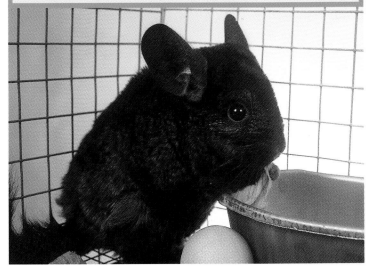

It seems that this ferret has taken variety a little far! Moderate variation is a good thing, however many of the foods we eat are not suitable for various small animals.

activity level of the pet will be a good indicator that the diet is either good, or in need of improvement. This feeding method assumes that the pet is not bored or stressed. Either of these conditions can result in syndromes that may cause excess eating or drinking, therefore making the trial and error method unreliable in such cases.

HOW MANY MEALS PER DAY?

If you make dry food accessible to your pet at all times, deciding how many fresh food meals are given becomes a matter of convenience. However, in most cases, the morning and one in the late afternoon or early evening should suffice.

If you are only going to feed once a day this meal should be given in the early evening. It is assumed that you will have time to spend with your pet, thus being able to observe its eating habits. Uneaten fresh foods should then be removed by the following morning.

Feeding is never an exact science, but providing a range of wholesome foods that offer excellent sustenance in a form

23

the pet finds interesting and enjoyable, should ensure a healthy pet. Meal time should never be reduced to being based on pure convenience. If this happens, all the enjoyment will be removed from what is an integral part of any animal's social life.

Never be afraid to do a little experimentation with foods. Where the less common pets are concerned be prepared to seek out as much information as you can. It often happens that some breeders and stores feed these pets on diets that are too restricted for long term good health, so you may need to play detective in order to find a diet that will keep your pet healthy and happy.

If you make dry food accessible to your pet at all times, it may only be necessary to feed him two fresh food meals a day. Check with your veterinarian or breeder for the best feeding schedule.

HAMSTERS

While there are about twenty-four hamster species only four are popular as pets. Hamsters are rodents, their closest relatives being mice, voles, rats, gerbils, and jirds. Most hamsters have no tail to speak of. This has certainly been one of the factors that, over the last fifty years, has enabled them to rise from obscurity to become a popular traditional pet.

The hamster species that elevated this small rodent to stardom is commonly known as the golden, or Syrian hamster. It is native to a very small region around Aleppo in northwestern Syria. There are three other species called golden hamsters, but these were not involved in the domestication process of the popular pet.

All domestic golden hamsters were developed from a single family that was captured in Syria in 1930 and bred in Israel. Some of the offspring were sent to European zoos and institutions. Offspring of these filtered into the pet trade, and a new animal hobby was in the making.

BASIC INFORMATION

The golden hamster is generally about 6.5 inches (16cm) long. He weighs about 113 grams (4 oz). The female has 14 or more teats, and the male none. The anogenital distance is greater in the male than in the female, who is usually larger than the male. They live for about two years.

Hamsters are sexually mature when they are about six weeks old, though they

Hamsters are popular traditional pets. They are native to a small region in Syria and have become domesticated over the last fifty years.

should be a few weeks older before being bred. The female's estrus cycle is approximately four days, the gestation period being 16 days. Litter size ranges from six to nine but can (rarely) be as many as 16.

PURCHASE AND CARE

The best time to purchase a hamster is when he is about six to ten weeks old. He will have been weaned at three weeks old, and should be very independent at that age. The key factors when buying a hamster are health and handling ease, the latter being essential.

Unlike most popular animals, the golden hamster should be kept as a single pet in its own housing. When either sex is kept together they may fight and inflict serious wounds on each other. Females are more aggressive, and must be carefully observed when paired to a male for mating.

Hamsters are basically herbivores, and numerous

Hamsters are basically herbivores, who will thrive on many commercially prepared foods with the addition of fresh fruits and vegetables.

commercially prepared foods are available for these pets. Fresh fruits and vegetables should be added, as well as small amounts of animal byproduct proteins. Avoid cold temperatures (below 60° F) as these may induce hibernation, but do not let the temperature rise much above 75° F, which may create heat stress.

COLOR PATTERNS

The color pattern of the wild hamster is white-bellied golden agouti, which means the golden color of the hamster is lightly ticked with dark hairs. Although still highly popular, with the passing of the years many color and pattern mutations have been developed. Today you can select from an extensive range that includes various whites, creams, browns, grays, and black. Some hamsters are red-eyed, others black-eyed. Patterns include the banded spotted, Dalmatian and tortoise shell.

Besides different colors and markings hamsters also are available in four coat types. A short sleek coat is most common, but there are three mutant forms. These are the longhaired, the satin (which is ultra sleek) and the rex, which is short and plush.

Hamsters are generally about 6.5 inches long and weigh about 4 ounces. Females are larger than males, and have a lifespan of up to two years.

Hamsters are bred in an extensive range of colors, including whites, creams, browns, grays, and blacks.

DWARF HAMSTERS

In recent years three species of dwarf hamsters have steadily gained in popularity. They are about half the size of the golden hamster and will live together in mixed or same sex pairs, even in groups, without undue fighting. The species are the Russian dwarf desert hamster, Roborovski's dwarf desert hamster, and the Chinese hamster.

Dwarf hamsters are generally white-bellied, gray-brown agouti rather than golden red. A satin mutation has been established and, under certain environmental conditions, a winter white coat may be displayed. The Chinese hamster has a longer tail. It's a delightful little pet and it may live for up to four years, or even longer. General care for these hamsters is the same for the golden. However, when being bred their gestation period is 21 days.

Hamsters make delightful pets. They are inexpensive to purchase, available in an extensive range of color patterns, and are easily housed within a considerable range of commercially made homes. They present no special diet problems or challenges and will prove to be a happy and interesting addition to your home.

Hamsters make delightful pets. They are inexpensive, easy to care for, and undemanding. They will prove charming additions to your home.

GERBILS

There are about 89 species of gerbils, otherwise known as jirds. They are relatives of hamsters, mice, rats and other small rodents. The popular pet species is commonly called the Mongolian gerbil, or Clawed jird. They are native to Siberia, Mongolia and China.

Gerbils gained popularity during the 1950s, originally introduced, like the hamster, as a laboratory animal. However, they make excellent pets. He is possibly the least likely of all small rodents to bite and can be kept in mixed pairs or small colonies. Same sex pairs are best if continual breeding is to be avoided. Opposite sexes will pair for life.

Well adapted to a desert existence, the gerbil's water consumption is minimal. This means less urine, which makes him a very clean pet. He is able to adapt to a wider range of temperatures than most small mammals. Probably the most inquisitive of small rodents, gerbils are always interesting to watch. They are also arguably the hardiest of small pets.

BASIC INFORMATION

The total length of a gerbil is about 6 inches (15 cm), including the furred tail. The male weighs about 3 ounces (85 g.), the female a little less. Sexes are distinguished by the greater anogenital distance in the male than in the female, and by the male's testes near the tail base. The hind legs are quite long, enabling gerbils to jump exceedingly well.

Gerbils are nocturnal creatures with acute hearing and sight, but will adapt to the daytime activity of their

Gerbils make excellent pets. They are gentle and inquisitive creatures that can be kept in mixed pairs or small groups.

owner. They typically live about three years, but up to five is possible. They reach sexual maturity about eight weeks old. The estrus period is typically four days while the gestation period is normally 25 days. Litter size is typically four to six, the offspring being weaned at 20 to 24 days of age.

PURCHASE AND CARE

The pet gerbil is best purchased at four to eight weeks old and should be handled with ease. Never pick them up by the rear half of the tail—this may cause injury and possible loss of part of the tail, which will not regenerate. Place fingers at the tail base, supporting the body weight with the other hand.

Gerbils are best kept in pairs because they are very social rodents. Should one of the pair die it may be difficult to introduce a new companion, so be aware of this fact and proceed with caution until a compatible friend is found.

Gerbils are also typically herbivores. Housing may also be similar to those for hamsters, the aquarium being a particularly good choice. However, be sure a secure lid is fitted, and that plenty of nesting material is supplied as these rodents enjoy burrowing. The average home temperature will be quite satisfactory for a gerbil.

COLOR

Gerbils are generally found in the wild as white-bellied agouti of gray-brown amply ticked with black guard hairs. A number of mutations have been established included black, blue, gray, cream, bicolor, lilac, dove, white, and Himalayan. Fur types include the short smooth fur of the wild gerbil and the mutated forms of longhaired, satin, and rex, each of which is available in various colors to provide a wide array of selections.

Although the gerbil has never been quite as popular as the hamster, it is, nonetheless, in some ways a superior pet, especially for small children. However, in some states gerbils are illegal. Make sure to check your local ordinances before making a purchase.

Gerbils live about three years and mate for life. They are very social animals that enjoy activity and will adjust well to their owner's schedule.

MICE AND RATS

Mice and rats have enjoyed popularity as pets since the 1700s. Although not everyone's cup of tea, they nonetheless still have devotees worldwide.

Mice and rats were probably the first rodent species to be kept as pets. Certainly the Chinese were skilled mice breeders many centuries ago. In Western countries these two rodents have been extremely popular pets since the late 1700's. The National Mouse Club of Britain was formed in 1895, giving mice a lineage that can compare with dogs, cats and rabbits.

Although no longer enjoying the same level of support as in past years—the arrival of hamsters, gerbils and other small mammals subtracting from their popularity—they nonetheless still have devotees worldwide, and remain contenders when choosing a small mammalian pet. In recent years, a number of rarely kept mouse species have even made considerable progress as exotic pets.

Rats are not to everyone's taste, and their association with plagues and other diseases has certainly been a key factor in restricting their popularity. However, the domestic rat is far removed from its wild ancestor and should not even be compared to him.

Rats are extremely clean pets and may well be one of the most intelligent smaller pets. Certainly, they should not be overlooked. Rats can become tame, companionable, and quite delightful to interact with.

There are hundreds of mice and rat species, but the ones most commonly seen in pet shops are the domesticated house mouse and the Norway or Brown rat.

BASIC INFORMATION

The mouse has a total length of about six inches (15cm) which includes the tail. Typical weight is about 1.1 ounces (31 g.). The rat is considerably larger having a

The domestic rat is far removed from his wild ancestors. He can become tame, companionable, and a joy to interact with.

total length of about 12 inches, weighing in at about 14 ounces (400 g.). In both animals males are larger than females.

Sexing is easily discovered by inspection of the anogenital distance, which is longer in the male than in the female. Additionally, the females have nipples and the males have testes near the tail base. The life span of mice is one to two years and generally about twice this in rats.

In both mice and rats the estrus cycle is about five days. Gestation is 19 to 21 days in the mouse and 21 to 23 days in rats. Litter size in mice is 6 to 12, while in the rat it is 7 to 14. Sexual maturity in mice is attained at about six weeks, in the rat at 10 or more weeks old. Youngsters are weaned at about three weeks of age.

PURCHASE AND CARE

Rats and mice are both very social creatures, so it's always best to obtain two so they will have a companion. Females make a better pair than males. However, if introduced at a young age, males will usually co-exist without fighting. However, males do secrete a stronger marking scent, so their housing must be kept scrupulously clean. Do not purchase one of each sex to share the same housing, otherwise you will be presented with one litter after another.

The ideal purchase age for either is at about four weeks old. Be sure that rats, in particular, display no sneezing or wheezy breathing, as this usually indicates a respiratory problem that is rarely cured. If such an individual is seen in a stock cage it is best to assume all other have the problem.

Mice and rats can be accommodated in any suitably sized small mammal housing, but the aquarium types are probably the best. Rats need a minimum sized cage of 24x12x12 inches (62x31x31 cm.). Avoid cages with all wire floors. Diet should be basically the same as for the hamster, but rats in particular need animal byproduct proteins. Commercially prepared rat mixtures and blocks are recommended.

COLORS AND PATTERNS

Both mice and rats are available in a wide range of

Rats are extremely clean pets and may very well be one of the most intelligent small mammals.

The average mouse is only about six inches long, including his tail, and weighs in at only one ounce! However, they do not lack in personality—extremely social creatures, it is best to keep mice in pairs.

Both mice and rats are available in a wide range of colors and patterns—especially the mouse, whose coat may be normal, satin, rex, or longhaired.

colors and patterns—especially the mouse, whose coat type may be normal, satin, astrex, rex, or longhaired. The rat's fur may be normal or rex. There is a Manx rat which is tailless, and there is even a hairless variety, but they require more care and are not recommended for first time owners.

Deciding between a mouse and a rat comes down to considerations concerning personal preference, as well as cost. The rat is more costly to obtain and care for. However, both pets are very intelligent and companionable. Whichever you choose will be a fascinating little pet that has proved itself over numerous centuries, with millions of owners.

Mice are social creatures. It's best to obtain two so they can play together.

GUINEA PIGS

If none of the mouse-like rodents appeal to you, and you feel you might prefer a somewhat larger pet, you can't go wrong with a guinea pig (cavy). These adorable pets have been kept in domesticity for about 3,000 years. They were probably introduced to Europe by the Spanish conquistadors, but it's only over the last half century or so they have really taken off as low cost, popular pets outside of their original homelands.

The domestic guinea pig is one of eight species of these native South American rodents. Externally tailless, these delightful critters are quiet, odorless, and rarely bite. They are very timid animals, best suited to homes where the children are gentle and eight years of age or older. They are large enough to be given some freedom, and will cohabit with rabbits without problems if carefully introduced.

BASIC INFORMATION

Guinea pigs are about 8 inches long (20 cm.) and typically weight about 2 lbs. (0.90 kg.) at adulthood. Sexing young stock is achieved by applying gentle pressure to either side of the genital opening. The penis of the male will protrude, while the opening of the female is covered by a membrane. In a mature male his testes will be more readily apparent.

Guinea pigs typically live about five years, though up to eight years is possible. Sexual maturity is reached within a few weeks with a male and by about three to four months in the female. However, they should not be bred until they are fix to six months old. The estrus period lasts about 16 days and the gestation period is typically is typically 63 to 68 days.

Litter size is usually three to four but can be much larger. The young are born fully furred and are running around and eating within hours.

The offspring are weaned at about three to four weeks of age. These pets are

Guinea pigs have been kept domestically for over 3,000 years. Introduced to the Europeans by the Spanish, their popularity in the States has really only increased over the last half century.

The domestic guinea pig is a delightful critter that is quiet, odorless, and gentle.

crepuscular (dawn and dusk) in their natural habitat, but adapt well to daytime lifestyle in captivity. Their hearing and scenting ability are acute.

PURCHASE AND CARE

Baby guinea pigs should be at least four to six weeks old before they are purchased to ensure they are fully independent of their mother. Sows (females) will live happily together, but boars (males) are best kept separately once mature. Do not mix the sexes, otherwise unwanted litters will be produced.

These pets are best housed indoors where the temperature will be controlled and suited to them. A commercial indoor pen or cage is the ideal accommodation. Ensure the floor is of slats, solid, or weld wire covered with a suitable plastic mat to protect their feet. Outdoor romps on nice days will be greatly

appreciated, provided they are confined to large fully enclosed exercise pens feature a small shelter.

Generally, guinea pigs are herbivores. However, the guinea pig cannot synthesize vitamin C. This must come via the diet in the form of vitamin C fortified commercial guinea pig foods, supplements of this vitamin, or daily fresh green foods in small quantities.

COLOR PATTERNS

The color pattern of the guinea pig found in the wild is an agouti gray-brown. Under domestic conditions many mutations have been established. Today, you can choose from an enviable range of colors and patterns, as well as from different hair types— normal (found in the wild), shorthaired, longhaired in two forms (Peruvian and Silkie [Sheltie in the UK]), rough coated in the form of the rosetted Abyssinian, and rex in the form of the Teddy (Rex in UK).

Additional breeds have been created by the satin gene, which gives an extra sheen to the coat, thus there is a normal smoothcoat and a satin smoothcoat. Finally, there is a created breed. Most of the breeds recognized in the US and UK are available

Guinea pigs are very timid animals, best suited to homes where they will be treated gently and given some freedom.

Guinea pigs are about eight inches long and weigh an average of two pounds. They live for anywhere from five to eight years.

in most colors creating a vast range of varieties from which you may choose your pet.

If your guinea pig is to be purely a house pet it is best you restrict your choice to the shorthaired or roughcoated breeds. The coats of the longhaired breeds will require considerable grooming if they are to be maintained in healthy condition. Ungroomed, the coat soon deteriorates into a tangled mass of tags, bits of food, and other detritus that make life for the pet very miserable.

The guinea pig is one of the best small pets you can purchase. Its many virtues and few drawbacks make it the ideal pet for anyone. All it needs is an owner who is especially considerate of its quiet and timid nature.

Baby guinea pigs should be at least four to six weeks old before they are purchased to ensure they are fully independent of their mother.

Guinea pigs are found in a dizzying array of colors, patterns, and hair types due to the many mutations that have been established.

RABBITS

Cheeky, inquisitive, cute, and thoroughly charming, rabbits have progressed from outdoor pets to indoor companions.

The rabbit is the most popular small-sized pet in the world. Cheeky, inquisitive, cute and thoroughly charming, it has progressed from an outdoor pet kept in a hutch to an indoor companion. The diminutive forms are enjoying enormous popularity, and a whole new hobby is developing around them as house pets.

Children find bunnies quite irresistible and adults have made them, after the dog and cat, the most popular exhibition mammal, and the most written about in children's stories, fables, and myths.

If you are seeking a lovable companion that is noiseless, immaculate in its appearance, inexpensive, easy to care for, and blessed with an amusing outgoing personality, then the rabbit is for you.

Rabbits were first domesticated in pre-Roman days. But not until Medieval times did they start to develop in a range of breeds and colors. Credit for this goes to religious monks. During the 19th century rabbits became

People find bunnies irresistible; they are the third most popular exhibition animal in the United States.

more and more fashionable as pets. Since that time the number of breeds, colors, and patterns have developed so tremendously that no other pet is seen in as many varieties.

The rabbit is not a rodent, but a member of the related order Lagomorpha, which includes hares and pikas. There are about 47 species of rabbits and hares. The domestic form was developed from a single species, commonly known as the Old World rabbit.

BASIC INFORMATION

Domestic rabbits are available in a wide range of weights from as small as two and half pounds (1.1 kg.) over 14 pounds (6.4 kg.). Sexing is achieved by inspection of the anogenital region. The distance between the anus and the genitals is greater in the male than in the female, though in very young stock distinction is more difficult to determine unless examined by an experienced hobbyist.

The average lifespan of a rabbit is about six to seven years, though some individuals may attain nine years, or more. Sexual maturity in the small breeds is achieved by three months of age, but in the large ones it may be six or more months. Rabbits may be bred at almost any time. The gestation period is typically 31 days.

A lovable noiseless animal, bunnies are immaculately clean, easy to care for, and are blessed with an outgoing personality.

Rabbits are available in a wide range of weights from as small as two and a half pounds to over 14 pounds.

Litter size in the small breeds is usually four to six, the larger breeds having up to ten as a normal maximum. The babies are weaned between four to eight weeks depending on the litter size and the breed.

PURCHASE AND CARE

Although a bunny may have been weaned at about four weeks old it is always preferable to purchase these pets when they are at least six to eight weeks of age. They are usually more independent, and better able to cope with the trauma of moving to a new home. If a small breed is the choice always check that the gnawing front incisor teeth are correctly aligned. This should be a routine check in all gnawing pets throughout their lives.

A commercially made indoor cage appropriately sized for the breed is the ideal housing. A bunny's diet should be comprised of quality branded pellets, mixed rabbit food (cereals and seeds), fresh green foods and fruits, as well as ample fresh hay, and of course, water.

Rabbits can be litter box trained. This requires plenty of patience and a number of litter boxes carefully located so one is never too far away for the bunny to use. Bunnies will make friends with dogs and cats, provided introductions are carefully supervised, and the bunny is never left alone.

There are over seventy breeds of rabbit to choose from. Be sure to learn about the individual breeds before making any decisions.

The Netherland Dwarf is among the most popular breed of rabbit in the United States and Britain.

You really can't go wrong with a rabbit as a pet. Be sure to select a breed that is an appropriate size for your home.

BREEDS & COLORS

There are over seventy rabbit breeds to choose from, some being much more popular and available than others. There are longhaired breeds (Angora types), normal haired, and of course the rex breeds, which sport a coat of plush velvet-like texture. Ear carriage may be erect or flop and long or short.

The range of colors and patterns is so extensive that you will simply be spoiled for choice. When these are combined with the different breeds the choice is bewildering. Currently, the most popular breeds in the US are the Mini Rex, Netherland Dwarf, Holland Lop, Mini Lop, Jersey Wooly, Californian, Dutch, French Lop, and the American Fuzzy Lop. Each of these, with the exception of the Californian and the French Lop, is a small or dwarf breed. In the UK, the Netherland dwarf and the lops are the most popular.

Unless you are prepared to devote ample time to grooming, it is best to restrict your initial choice to the breeds that have normal or rex coats. This said, grooming the longhaired dwarf breeds is not a major chore if it's done on a regular basis.

You really can't go wrong with a rabbit for a pet. Be sure that you select a breed that is an appropriate size for your home. Sometimes it is best to begin with a purebred because their size is predictable. Otherwise, enjoy your bunny for the interesting and loveable pet he is.

HEDGEHOGS

At any one point in time, here will always be many "exotic" pets that hobbyist maintain. However, rarely do any of these attain the sort of following that enable them to become fully domesticated.

The African pygmy hedgehog is one of the very rare exceptions.

At this time it is so well on its way to joining the ranks of the hamster, gerbil, and guinea pig as a traditional

When hedgehogs first arrived in the early 1990s, they cost thousands of dollars each! Now they are no more expensive than a purebred dog, or less, depending on where you live.

Rarely do exotic pets attain the sort of popularity that allows them to become fully domesticated.

At this time, the hedgehog is well on his way to joining the ranks of traditional pets. In a few years he will no longer even be regarded as exotic.

pet, that in a few years will no longer be regarded as exotic. Indeed, if the hedgehog becomes your choice as a pet it will have been bred in captivity, from a number of domestic generations.

At first costing as much as a thousand dollars each in the early 1990's, a nice hedgehog can now be purchased for no more than the cost of a purebred dog or cat, and often much less, depending on the locality you live in.

Although, with their prickly spines, hedgehogs look like pocket-sized relatives of the porcupines, they are not. Actually, the guinea pig is more closely related to a porcupine than is a hedgehog. These pets are members of

the order Insectivore which contain some 390 species.

They are the first members of this order to gain popularity as a pet. Essentially nocturnal, they will adapt to daytime activity, but should be protected from strong sunlight.

Although all of the fourteen species of hedgehogs have been kept under domestic conditions, the African pygmy, or White-bellied species, is the one the hobby has developed around, and which the following text is dedicated to.

BASIC INFORMATION

The hedgehog is typically seven to eight inches (18-20 cm.) in length. The tail is very short and virtually hairless. Average weight is 11 to 16 ounces (312-454 g.). The upper body and crown is covered with short spines that may be held upright, placed in a criss-cross position, or

The hedgehog is generally seven to eight inches in length and weighs about 11 to 16 ounces. His upper body and crown are covered with long, sharp spines. His face, chest, and underbelly are covered with soft fur.

laid flat—depending on whether the individuals mood. When in full defense the hedgehog curls into a tight ball, presenting its adversary with a mass of sharp spines. The face, chest, and underbelly are covered with soft fur.

The teeth are small, but sharp, and can inflict a painful wound. Only very well socialized individuals should be considered as pets.

Sexing is very easily determined. The penis is seen where you would find a navel button—in the middle of the abdomen. The female genitals are located close to the anus. The lifespan of this pet will normally be five to seven years, rarely longer. Sexual maturity may be attained as early as eight weeks of age, but breeding is not recommended with individuals under six months old.

Hedgehogs will breed throughout the year under suitable conditions. The gestation period is 35 to 37 days and the offspring are weaned at four to six weeks old. Litter size is typically four to six, but larger litters are possible. Cannibalism and abandonment are not uncommon in stock that is poorly managed and in under-sized housing.

PURCHASE AND CARE

First check that this pet can legally be kept in your state. The recommended purchase age is eight weeks or older. It's essential the youngster is very hand tame. Any that are not should be rejected. Be aware that strange scents can prompt these pets to nip, especially if they are not familiar with being handled. Two females will live amicably together. Much more caution should be taken with two males as they often fight unless reared together from babyhood.

Housing should have a solid floor, and preferably solid walls, because these pets will try to climb bars and can be injured if their claws become entangled. Mini-ecosystems with wall heights of twelve or more inches are the ideal housing. Include a nestbox. Avoid cedar wood shavings—they can create respiratory and other problems. Commercial plant fiber floor covering is the best.

Ideal temperatures range from 68 to 74° F. Below 50° F may induce torpor and hibernation. High

Like other small mammals, hedgehogs enjoy some activity to pass the time. It's important when choosing a playwheel to make sure it's specially designed for hedgehogs so their feet won't fall through the bars. Photo courtesy of Balanced Innovations.

Unlike other small mammals, hedgehogs eat meat and insects. Their diets should consist of small amounts of fruit and vegetables, but mainly mealworms and other foods of animal origin.

temperatures will induce heat stress.

Unlike other small mammals hedgehogs are carnivorous and insectivorous in their diet. They will eat only tiny amounts of fruit and vegetable matter. Egg yolk, scrambled egg, chicken and beef are typical items, along with a few mealworms and quality dry cat foots. Correctly reared they will also eat cheese, some boiled white fish, and other foods of animal origin.

Strange scents will elicit a habit known as self-anointing in which the hedgehog will deposit a foamy substance on its body—this is a normal behavior. They should be supplied with a dust bath in which to roll. This is their way of keeping the skin in good health.

COLOR PATTERN

The normal (wild) color pattern of the hedgehog is agouti spires over white-cream underparts. A dark mask is typical, but light examples are also seen. An albino mutation (white with pink eyes), as well as bicolor (black and white), have been established. Light agouti forms are often called cream or cinnamon. Such terms can be misleading as they imply mutation which may not be the case. A black-eyed white is also report.

A well hand tamed pet is a delight to own and can be handled with no fear of being spiked or bitten. Hedgehogs are not recommended for young children or owners who are not prepared to give them the extra attention they need in handling and correct care. However, with attention, care, and patience the hedgehog can be a most enjoyable pet.

A tamed hedgehog is a delight to own and can be handled with no fear of being bitten or spiked. With attention, care, and patience the hedgehog can be a most enjoyable pet.

SUGAR GLIDERS

Following in the footsteps of the hedgehog as being both the first of its order to gain in-home pet status and an exotic animal that's a rising star is the sugar glider. This small furry bundle hails from Australia, New Guinea, and surrounding islands.

The sugar glider is a marsupial, so it has a pouch in which the offspring develop and are reared to weaning age. Arboreal and nocturnal by nature, these gliders can leap from a high point and glide with ease across a room to land elsewhere—including you if they are very tame and secure in your presence. They are certainly unusual, and will appeal to those looking for a pet that's a little different, but have the time to offer them care for their special requirements.

The sugar glider is a marsupial, so it has a pouch in which offspring develop until weaning age.

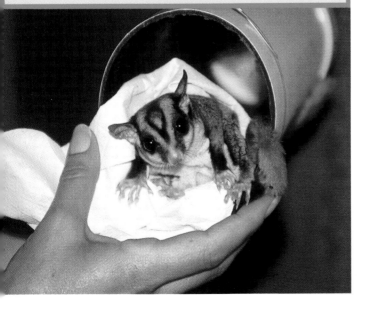

Fast becoming a rising star in the pet world, the exotic animal known as the sugar glider hails from Australia and New Guinea.

BASIC INFORMATION

Body length is typically about nine to twelve inches (24-31 cm.) half of which is comprised by a bushy tail. A male weighs about 4.8 ounces (135 g.), the female being slightly smaller. Sexes are distinguished by inspecting the lower abdominal region when a round, somewhat swollen, area will be evident or missing. If present this is a male. The female's pouch is only seen when she is in breeding condition. There are five digits on each foot, all clawed except the inner toe of the hind feet, which is adapted for gripping branches and tree trunks.

The gliding membrane stretches from the front to the back legs and is easily seen as a fold of skin when the pet is moving around in its housing. The color pattern found in the glider is gray agouti upper parts with cream cheeks, chest and underbelly. There are black-brown stripes on the head, and a stripe running down the back. A scent gland is often readily seen on the crown of males. The typical lifespan of a sugar glider will be about 10 years.

Sexual maturity is reached at eight to ten months old in the female, somewhat later in the male. The estrus cycle of the female is about 29 days and the gestation period is just 16 days. However, the offspring then crawls into the pouch where it will develop.

It commences leaving the pouch at about 70 days old and is usually weaned by the age of 16 weeks. Litter size is normally one or two. These pets may live in a family

Certainly unusual, you must have the time to offer sugar gliders care for their special requirements.

colony, in pairs or trios (one male to two females) or all females. Being very social by nature a single individual needs plenty of interaction with its owner, or the companionship of its kind.

PURCHASE AND CARE

First of all, check that sugar gliders can legally be kept in your state. The ideal purchase age is when the glider is fully weaned and is living independent of its mother. This means about 18-20 weeks of age, to be on the safe side. The male has a

These little creatures can leap from a high point and glide with ease across a room to land elsewhere—including on you!

Sugar gliders need to be protected from other pets in the home. It is particularly important that they not be frightened during the first few weeks in your family.

These pets should be given ample exercise time outside of their housing. Be careful to ensure there are no dangers when they leap from one location to another.

stronger scent than the female, but this aside either sex will make a fine pet. Be sure he's hand tame, this being especially important with the more mature individuals.

Housing should be as large as possible with good height so the glider can climb about in branches within. Indoor aviaries would be the ideal home, but tall finch cages can be smaller alternatives. Place a nestbox high up in the cage so the pet will feel secure. A feeding platform and a water dispenser will complete basic furnishings.

Sugar gliders are omnivorous feeders. They require a diet that includes foods of plant and animal origins. A typical ratio will be 25-35% animal protein (meats and invertebrates—such as mealworms) and 65-75% fruit, vegetables, and grain and other seeds. Offer a wide ranging menu to establish favored items.

These pets should be given ample exercise time outside of their housing. Ensure there are no dangers when they leap from one location to another, such as open windows, or dogs, cats or other pets that might attempt to bite or claw at them. Children must handle these timid and somewhat delicate pets with great care. Avoid cold or drafty housing locations, as well as excessively hot conditions.

Sugar gliders make delightful pets, but they can be a little messy, and do have more of a scent than some other pets. Meticulous cleaning of their housing is therefore essential due to the more liquid state of their fecal matter.

They enjoy climbing up drapes and other furnishings to attain a high vantage point. They are inquisitive critters and very amusing to observe. More expensive than hedgehogs, but still competitively priced, they require a somewhat more dedicated owner than do the very popular pets.

FERRETS

If you have ever owned a dog or cat and would now like a pet that although very different, shares dogs' and cats' outgoing personalities, then the ferret is perfect for you. They are most closely related to the other species of weasels, ermines, stoats, minks, and polecats. They are generally inexpensive, depending on their quality and color. Ferrets are thought to be the domestic form of the European polecat. They were first bred in captivity over 2,500 years ago.

> The ferret is a perfect pet for someone who enjoys the outgoing personality of a dog, but would like something a little different. The ferret was first bred in captivity over 2,500 years ago!

Originally an exterminator of snakes, mice, and rats, the ferret later became highly popular for use in the sport of rabbiting, where he was used to flush rabbits from their burrow. In this capacity the ferret is still used extensively in many European countries.

Today, the ferret is also a highly popular pet with many attributes. He is very intelligent, inquisitive, lovable, and will never cease to amuse you—as well as constantly try to outwit you with his antics and mischievous exploits. They can be real rascals when it comes to delving into drawers and cupboards, stealing clothing, and other things that may appeal. Ferrets love to take naps in the most unlikely places, such as open washing machines, drawers, lockers, and other places where it might easily and inadvertently get locked in! Owning a ferret is an experience best suited to someone who will love a cheeky and playful pet.

BASIC INFORMATION

The total body length of a male (known as a hob), on average, is about 15 inches (38 cm.) and the tail is about five to six inches (12.7-15 cm.). The male ferret weighs two to three pounds (0.91-1.4 kg.). He is about 25% larger and heavier than the female. The actual weight range in these pets may vary considerably, and normally rises during the winter months.

Sexing is based on the anogenital distance, which is

about twice as long in the male than in the female. Both sexes have nipples (4 pairs is normal). There are five clawed toes on each foot. The typical lifespan will be seven to ten years.

The female ferret (known as a jill) is an induced ovulator. The estrus period for a female ferret is continuous until she has mated or it is the end of the breeding season. Gestation is typically 42 days and the litter size is normally six to nine. Ferret babies, known as kits, are weaned at six to eight weeks old.

PURCHASE AND CARE

Ferrets may be kept legally in most states—but check your local ordinances to make sure. Never obtain kits that are younger than eight to twelve weeks of age. It's essential that your ferret is neutered; this will remove much of its musky body scent, and will help to avoid potentially lethal problems related to the vulva in unmated females. Vaccinations against canine distemper, rabies and other diseases are strongly recommended for the ferret. However, check with your veterinarian.

A ferret's housing should be spacious. An indoor rabbit hutch with nestbox will do, or similar secure commercial home designed for ferrets or comparably sized mammals. A solid floor is best, but a mesh floor is acceptable as long as it is fitted with a good floor

The ferret is a highly popular pet known for his inquisitive and lovable nature, as well as his unending desire to amuse.

The total body length of a male ferret is about 15 inches long with a five- to six-inch tail. They generally weigh up to three pounds, males being about 25% larger than females.

Ferrets are nosy to a delightful fault. Use your ferret's curiosity to teach it unusual tricks.

mat. Tiered ferret homes are popular. A litter box should be supplied. Avoid clay litters—use the non-dusty environmentally friendly types.

The ferret's diet should contain about 35% meat protein and 30% fat. A commercial ferret food is useful as a staple, but quality meat (cooked or raw), chicken, and occasionally white fish should be added for variety. Cat food will also be appreciated, while raw or boiled eggs are good for a one-a-week treat. At least two meals a day are necessary—the more the better since they have such rapid metabolisms.

COLOR PATTERN

There is now a wide range of colors and patterns of ferrets to choose from. Originally, the all white, pink-

Ferret housing should be spacious, with a solid floor and litter box. Tiered ferret homes have become very popular with pets and owners; they allow the ferret freedom of movement even while confined.

There is now a wide range of colors and patterns of ferrets to choose from. Originally, the albino was most popular. Today sables, Siamese, silver mitts, silvers, and almost black ferrets are the favored choices.

eyed albino was the most popular. But today the sables, Siamese, silver mitts, silvers and almost black ferrets are the favored choices of pet owners.

The ferret is a gorgeous and very companionable pet if obtained as a youngster and carefully reared. It may nip while it's a baby and should never be subjected to poor handling by children because it can inflict a painful bite.

Once tame, ferrets can be exercised on a harness and lead (better than a collar) and will beguile you with their charm and playfulness. Two ferrets make great pals for each other. However, keep them away from pets such as rabbits, guinea pigs, and hamsters or they may end up as a meal!

CHINCHILLAS

Of all the domestic pets you may keep, only one has a coat more plush and soft than that of the rex coated rabbit. It's the chinchilla. Its fur is not a mutation but needed to ward off the cold in its high Andes homeland of South America.

Now classified as a very endangered species in its natural habitats, the chinchilla is bred by the millions under domestic conditions for its valuable pelt—the most costly of any animal. But they have also become popular pets, and justifiably so. A tame individual is very charming, playful and easy to care for.

There are just two wild species of chinchilla. Their name is derived from the Spanish for the animal, which is probably derived from the Quechuan language of the Incas.

With its large eyes and ears, bushy tail, and velvet-like fur, the chinchilla is large enough to be handled easily, yet is only the size and weight of the smallest of rabbits. This makes for a delightful pet for all ages.

First and foremost the chinchilla is known for its outrageously soft, plush coat. Its fur is not a mutation, but a necessity to ward off the cold in its native South America.

BASIC INFORMATION

The body length of a chinchilla is about 12 inches (32 cm.) and the tail is about 5 inches long (13 cm.). It can weigh up to 1.7 pounds (0.8 kg.) for a female, which is the larger sex, and to 1.1 pounds (0.5 kg.) for a male. Sexing is via inspection of the anogenital region, which is much longer in the male than in the female. The lifespan is exceptional for a pet rodent and will typically be about 15 years, though some have attained over 20.

When breeding, the estrus period is 38 days, gestation period is normally 111 days or longer, and litter size is two to four offspring. These are born fully furred with eyes open. They are weaned at six to eight weeks old.

Chinchillas have become very popular pets, and justifiably so, because when tame they are charming, playful, and easy to care for.

PURCHASE AND CARE

The minimum recommended age of purchase is eight or more weeks old. It's essential that the pet be friendly and easily handled because these rodents are large enough to inflict a painful bite.

Housing should be spacious and with a solid or matted floor. Include a nestbox and a dust bath. The bath is very important for these pets in order to keep their fur clean and in a healthy state—the dust power can be obtained from pet shops. A litter box is useful if the cage is large enough.

A chinchilla is about 12 inches long with a tail of five inches, and weighs about 1.7 pounds, the female being the larger sex.

Be sure to have your chinchilla examined by a vet at the first sign of illness. Most small animals—and chinchillas are no exception—do not show symptoms until they are quite ill, so speed is of the essence.

Climbing branches are good, as well as block of wood to gnaw on. Avoid cedar shavings, corn cob litter and white pine.

The chinchilla diet should consist of formulated pellets, augmented with fresh hay, and small amounts of fruits and vegetables. Be careful that the temperature does not rise much above 70°F as this may induce heat stress. Their

There are just two species of chinchilla known in the wild. They have been hunted to near extinction for their valuable pelts.

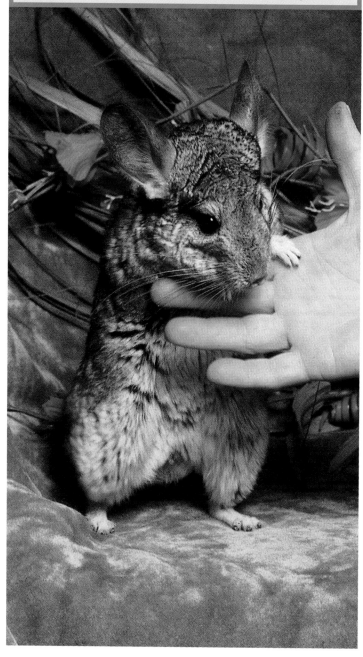

With its large eyes and oversized ears, bushy tail, and velvet-like fur the chinchilla makes a delightful pet for all ages.

dense fur (over sixty hairs per follicle) keeps them warm—and largely free of external parasites.

COLOR AND PATTERN

The chinchilla color pattern found in the wild is a silver gray that is actually an agouti if the hairs are inspected. A number of mutations have been established including albino, white, silver, black, charcoal, brown, beige, blue and various shaded patterns. Some are much more costly than others.

The chinchilla, while popular, has not yet attained its potential. A strong interest in exhibition is now developing. This is a pet definitely worth considering, which combines intelligence with good looks, a great personality, and a very impressive lifespan.

Waiting In The Wings

All the pets discussed in his book have already gained a degree of popularity. This chapter will briefly cover four other small mammals that are waiting in the wings for their turn at stardom. They are already kept by many hobbyists, but still remain largely unknown to most pet owners.

You may have to special order them from your pet shop, or seek out a dealer that specializes in exotic pets. In all instances you must check that they can legally be kept in your state and locality.

It is strongly recommended that any exotic pet has been bred under domestic conditions so it's well socialized and perfectly healthy. Imported wild specimens should not be purchased as pets.

FAT-TAILED GERBIL OR DUPRASI

The fat-tailed gerbil is indigenous to the desert regions of Morocco and Egypt. It's a small stockily built rodent with a soft, but dense coat and a furry club-shaped tail. It's very different in appearance from most other gerbils. The fat-tailed gerbil's diet is insectivorous and herbivorous. The usual lifespan is about $4^1/_2$ years. They have definite potential for greater popularity.

STRIPED GRASS MICE

There are eight species of striped mice. They vary in the

The fat-tailed gerbil is a new entry into the ever-expanding small mammal hobby. Very different in appearance from the traditional gerbil below, they have definite potential for great popularity.

The African pygmy hedgehog was once considered an exotic animal and is now kept by many as a pet. As long as there are hobbyists exploring new breeds there will always be pets waiting in the wings for their turn at stardom.

number of stripes and broken stripes (spots) running horizontally along their bodies. All are African in origin. Their body size is generally 4 inches (10 cm.) with a tail about the same length. Their color is shades of brown, with beige spots and cream to gray underbelly. They weight about 2 ounces (57 g.).

Their diet is herbivorous, as for most mice. The lifespan in captivity is typically about three years. They are all inexpensive to purchase and make an interesting alternative to regular domestic mice.

DEGU

This South African rodent has a body of about 6 inches (15 cm.) in length with a tail two-thirds as long as the body. He weights about 7 ounces (200 g.). They are very common in Chile. Their color is a gray-brown agouti with an orange case, underparts are cream and the tail tip is black.

Their diet is herbivorous and a dust bath is needed. These are fascinating and interesting pets that somewhat resemble the chinchilla, but are not as large.

SHORT-TAILED OPOSSUMS

This is one of 17 species of these South American marsupials. However, it does not develop a pouch (marsupium). With an elongated body and tapered snout this pet is about 6 inches long (15 cm.), and has an almost naked tail of about 2.5 inches (6 cm.).

They range in color from gray to brown-red agouti. They are omnivorous and are predators of rodents and insects, including scorpions, in their homelands of Brazil, Bolivia and Paraguay. Those who own these small marsupials say they make excellent pets once hand-tame.

HEALTH CARE FOR ALL ANIMALS

The principles of maintaining good health, and minimizing the risk of serious illnesses, are common to all pet species. A knowledge of specific diseases and their treatment is by no means necessary to either the pet owner or breeder, but it may be useful. However, it can tempt some owners to make diagnoses that could be very wrong. Any treatment based on such a diagnosis could be potentially lethal—especially as most of modern drugs should only be used under veterinary advice.

The hobbyist is better served by concentrating all efforts into ensuring breeding standards are the highest order so that problems are avoided rather than treated. This may seem a well worn cliché, but it is highly effective

Your pet's micro-climate has a tremendous effect on his health. Make sure to monitor temperature as well as cleanliness to ensure that your pet is living in a stress-free environment.

under all normal conditions. Here, the subject will only be briefly reviewed, but it should give you a valuable reference base.

A first step for any hobbyist in making sure that the animal he purchases is healthy is to ensure that the highest breeding standards are adhered to. This will avoid problems before they begin.

THE MICRO-CLIMATE

The cage or other housing in which your pet is living is called its micro-climate. While this may be in the same room in which you are living, which is the general environment, it can be very different in its climatic composition. Just one example will illustrate this aspect.

Byproducts of digestion are fecal matter and urine. These release ammonia into the air. Within the general environment the quantity of this may be only a few parts per million (ppm). If it were to be in excess of 25 ppm this would be regarded as clinically dangerous to humans. Within an uncleaned cage it can easily exceed 100 ppm.

You would only notice this when you approached the cage, but the smell would be offensive to you. Imagine the effect it is having on a small pet that must live constantly in it. The decomposition of fecal matter and other debris, which would include uneaten fresh foods, dramatically increases the potential for dangerous bacteria to multiply.

Not surprisingly, under these conditions, a pet's immune system eventually becomes incapable of coping, and illness is the result. These risks can be removed if total cleaning of the entire housing is attended to at least once a week, or more often if the housing is small and the conditions indicate this is necessary.

Be sure that after cleaning that involves chemicals (dilutions of disinfectants or bleach) the cage is rinsed to remove all traces of these. They can be dangerous to small pets. Also, remember housing must be dry before the pet is placed back into it.

CHECK-UPS

A pet should be physically examined each time it is handled. The sooner a problem is noticed, the sooner it can be effectively treated. The fur should be carefully inspected for signs of external parasites and the teeth checked for correct length and alignment. Any of the following may indicate poor health: weeping eyes, runny nose, discharge of pus from the nose or eyes, swollen nostrils, closed or partially closed eyes, any swelling, abrasions or sores, flaky skin, loss of hair—bald patches, diarrhea, and blood-streaked urine or fecal matter.

Not all illnesses manifest themselves in external signs, so behavioral changes from the norm may be the only clue that you will get of something amiss. These include the following: general lethargy, sitting hunched in a corner, twitching of muscles, excessive scratching, sickness, labored and/or wheezy breathing, sudden erratic movements, abnormal reluctance to being handled, and indications of pain when being handled.

TEETH ALIGNMENT

It is vital that the incisor teeth of all rodents and lagomorphs (which include rabbits) are maintained at the correct length. If their

Any changes in the behavior of your small mammal may indicate illness. A thorough veterinary exam will be necessary in these instances.

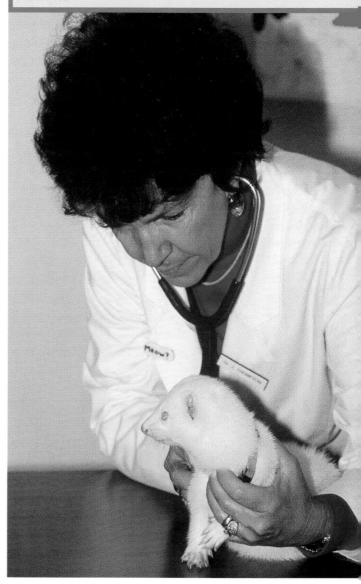

alignment is normal the upper teeth will just overlap those of the lower jaw. By rubbing against each other, and by gnawing on hard foods, such as pellets, small branches of wood and their like, they are kept in good condition.

However, the alignment can be abnormal through injury, tugging on cage bars out of boredom, or because the pet is of poorly bred stock. In these instances the teeth do not wear as they should, and grow in a natural curve. Eventually, the pet is unable to eat, and the teeth may actually pierce the jaw. This must never be allowed to happen.

Check the alignment when the pet is purchased, and continue to inspect the teeth through the pet's life. If a problem becomes apparent your vet can trim and file the teeth periodically.

It is vital that the incisor teeth of all small mammals be maintained.

If you suspect a pet is ill never delay taking action. Often times small mammals deteriorate rapidly. Fortunately, in most instances they will recover quickly with the help of a good veterinarian and some medication.

WHAT TO DO IF YOU THINK YOUR PET IS ILL

If you suspect a pet is ill never delay in taking action. Small species in particular can deteriorate rapidly—but can just as quickly recover if treatment is prompt. Make a note of the signs that give cause for concern. You should at least telephone your vet and relate the signs.

They may only represent a tummy upset, a chill, or other conditions that will rectify itself within 24 hours. But, especially if two or more signs are evident, you may be witnessing the first outward signs of a major problem, condition, or disease.

Also, check the conditions in the housing, especially those related to cleanliness, foods, and the temperature. The housing should be stripped down and thoroughly cleaned. Check that the food is not sour, contaminated or, in the case of seed and grain, split or oozing a liquid—this is dangerous.

Are all foods being correctly stored in cool, dry, darkened cupboards that are vermin free? These clues will be imprint in the vet's diagnosis of the problem.

EXTERNAL PARASITES

In an effort to eradicate parasites from your pet, its housing, or the general environment, many owners may inadvertently create problems. For example, constant use of quick action aerosol sprays to kill house flies can be very dangerous to the respiratory and other systems of small pet mammals.

Most small pets are fastidious self groomers and the use of some topical parasiticides can be dangerous or even fatal to a pet. They build up in the body destroying beneficial and disrupting correct body cell metabolism. This is especially so in hedgehogs. They have larger than normal fat deposits because they are hibernating or estivating species. The chemicals in the treatments become deposited in the fat layer.

The choice of the most appropriate treatment for external parasites on the pet is best left to your vet who is more aware of the dangers related to given treatments. Never use two or more different treatments concurrently—it can be risky at the least.

So, if you have maintained high levels of husbandry, how then do pets still contract major diseases? The answer is the pathogens can arrive via very many ways. They be transported on your clothes, on your hands (as after gardening or handling pets in a friend's home), after visits to animal exhibitions, via other pets in the home (such as dogs or cats), via the food, and of course simply by airborne means.

Spores can be transported vast distances in the air. They can lie dormant in your home just waiting for any breakdown in husbandry standards because these provide the right conditions for their maturation and proliferation.

Your pet does not live under laboratory conditions, so it's always at risk to pathogens. Your diligence in all aspects of husbandry will minimize the potential illness, and increase the potential for any problems to be treated effectively should a worse case scenario become a reality.

Grooming your pet is another aspect of maintaining a healthy animal. Regular grooming will enable you to eradicate all external parasites.

Pets will always be at risk of pathogens; however, vigilance in maintaining healthy breeding stock will result in strong offspring that will not fall prey to illnesses easily.